How to Start Investing in the Philippine Stock Market? – A step by step Beginner's Guide

ELTON JOHN T. AGUILAR

Copyright © 2012 Elton John T. Aguilar

All rights reserved.

ISBN-13: 978-1480013858

ISBN-10: 1480013854

DEDICATION

Dedicated to my mother and father.

CONTENTS

	Acknowledgments	i
Step 1	Be Motivated to Invest	1
Step 2	Know the Facts	13
Step 3	Select the Stock Broker	16
Step 4	Apply for a Trading Account	19
Step 5	Make a Trading Plan	25
Step 6	Start Trading	28

ACKNOWLEDGMENTS

Thanks to God Almighty, for the blessings

Thanks to my ever caring family, for the support

Thanks to COL Financials,
Philippine Stock Exchange,
Investopedia,
for the information materials

Thanks to followers
of PhilStockNews.blogspot.sg,
for the encouragement

STEP 1 BE MOTIVATED TO INVEST

At some point in my adult life that I came to realize, "I am getting old and have not yet made concrete preparations for my retirement". It dawn upon me that I am still dependent on the company's savings plan and the Social Security System (SSS). Hearing from the financial news that these type of saving system no longer can feed an increasing lifestyle when retirement age comes. Companies can go bust or bought out. Work is no longer permanent. Outsourcing, contract and part-time employment is now the trend. SSS entitlement depends on how the government managed those funds and from past studies, it seems not quite performing good.

After a long soul searching and thorough evaluation of my financial status, I decided to myself that I need to be motivated to not only save but to invest for my future. I need to be prepared if all savings and investing plans provided by the company or government fails. There is no other person to help financially but me. This is a pessimistic view.

In the brighter side, additional passive income can go a long mile. It can finance in building more businesses, thus hiring more people. It can be used to setup condominiums, resorts and apartments, thus allowing more people to have roof over their heads. It can fund more infrastructure projects like roads, bridges and parks for quality lifestyle of the people.

Along this line of thinking, I evaluated which investment vehicle to invest. There were available investment vehicles to choose from: bank deposits, bonds, real estate and stocks.

After some evaluation of my investment portfolio, I recognized that the stock market is one of the investment vehicles that is right for me. Being knowledgeable of the Philippines and with its economy is on the fast recovery from the 2008 financial crisis, I chose the Philippine Stock Market.

I am writing this book for people planning to start investing in the Philippine Stock Market and have no clue where to start. This book is for you.

This book is also for you if you are planning to start investing in the Philippine Stock Market who are:

- Overseas Foreign Workers (OFW) looking to invest cash remittances
- Foreign Investors planning to invest in the Philippine Stock Market
- Local Filipinos planning to invest in stocks

Why the need to Be Motivated to Invest?

First thing you have to do is be motivated to invest. Without the burning fire of motivation, you will have no reason to move on or even to start with. Your motivation might be for your family, yourself or for others. Any burning motivation will propel you to success.

Motivation can be your childhood dreams, goals in life for you personally or your family. Recognize these things and embrace with faith that these will come true. According to 'The Secret' book, "The entire universe will conspire to fulfill your dreams". All you must do is just keep motivated.

A journey starts with knowing your destination. Knowing where you are going and believing it can be achieved, will be your fuel to keep on moving forward to take it step by step and enjoying each moment of your trip.

How about you, what motivates you to invest? I would like you to ponder on this question for a while and list the things or people who motivates you to invest.

Why should you invest your money?

The money you invest today will generate future purchasing power that will keep you ahead of inflation and provide a sense of financial security. Your financial goals at different time horizons maybe buying a house, paying for your child's college education and setting aside for your own retirement.

The available invested funds can fulfill your dreams and goals.

Let your money work for you and not the other way around. Every income you receive, take some of it as savings. This saved money will now be your worker. Let them work by itself through compounding. How? You must invest your money.

Investing your money for passive income. Passive income is money received from investment vehicles for investing money to those money-making machines. Investing in stocks is one of those investment vehicles. Compounding will work if you re-invest that passive income. This is an easy and sure way to great wealth.

I encourage you to have savings. The more of money saved the better. This saved money will be your capital to invest.

Take a look at your investment portfolio. How much money are working for you? How much passive income is coming periodically? Be honest with your checking. If you have no money invested yet, do not be worried. There is a way to start up your capital for investing.

What is the best way to start investing?

The best way to start investing is by saving money. Always pay yourself first. Every time you receive cash through salary or profits from your business, set aside some of the money and invest it. I encourage you to write a check to your investment account first before any other expenses. Remember that consistency of this practice and not missing a beat is the right way to make it work.

From now on, you need to discipline yourself that any income you receive, you will take some of it immediately for yourself as savings. Repeat these to yourself, "I must pay myself first for every income I receive." And as Nike say, "Just do it!"

Minimum cash to invest in the Philippine stock market is Five Thousand pesos. So you can allot Five Thousand pesos or more from your savings to invest monthly on buying stocks.

This invested money will now work for you with little to no active effort on your part. But you will reap rewards that is passive income when the stock appreciates or dividends are provided.

Do not withdraw from your savings and investment accounts. Let it grow to a gigantic portfolio and soon you will realize that it can now feed your lifestyle.

But first, you need to cultivate the value of saving. A farmer do not eat all his harvested crops, but set aside some for next planting season. This is another form of saving to invest in farming. You will not butcher all your farm animals for meat, but set aside some for reproduction. This is saving to invest in animal raising.

Same with money, set aside some as savings to invest.

Make a savings plan. How much is my income? How much can I save? Pay yourself first. Write a check or deposit of those saved money to your investment account. Do not withdraw your savings or investment portfolio to let it grow. Just do it!

Why invest in the stock market?

There are two ways to make your saved money grow when invested in the stock market:

1. Increase in stock price or capital appreciation

2. Dividends declared by the company

The stock you bought can increase in price due to market supply and demand sentiments or a new price appreciation for the company's capital status. This profit from the increase in price is still in paper and can be realized when sold at a higher price from its purchased price. You can buy and hold the stocks for long term to allow the invested money appreciate. You can also sell the stocks for quick profit.

Dividends are the proceeds from the company's earnings that is shared back to the investors. It can be in the form of cash, stock offer, or any other item of value. You can use the dividends to buy another stock. You can also roll over those dividends back to compound.

Another way to invest is to buy bulk shares in order to buy out the company and be the major stockholder resulting to be the new owner of the company. This is another way to own the business itself and have control, rather than building start-up business. These listed companies have proven record in the business and financial statements are publicly available for investors to evaluate. Most of the tycoons are buying shares on listed companies. Mr. Lucio Tan has multiple majority shares and control in multiple companies. Holding companies also have majority stake and control on multiple companies across industries. Ayala Corporation (AC) is an example of such holding firm.

Make a decision to invest in the Philippine Stock Market. You can start to prepare now by going PSE website www.pse.com.ph. Browse the listed companies, the Index list, and market information.

Before you go to battle, you must know the terrain; know your enemy and allies, and what you need to achieve. In stock investing, know your market, know the listed companies (which one can be your allies), so you can invest on those listed companies having a good track record.

This book will give you step by step guide as beginners to investing in the Philippine Stock Market. Keep on reading and more goldmine of information you will treasure.

When is the right time to invest?

When investing, time is your most precious asset. The longer your time horizon is, the more time you have to make your money grow. Compounding is a multiplier effect that occurs when earnings or dividends on your investment begin to generate their own earnings.

Those who start investing sooner rather than later have a tremendous advantage. If money is invested in good quality stocks over the long-term and then reinvest the dividends earned as your receive then, your investment grows exponentially over time.

The right time to invest is NOW.

STEP 2 KNOW THE FACTS

Yes! I am excited and motivated to start investing in the Philippine Stock Market. But, "What do I need to know about stocks, stock market, the Philippine Stock Market, Listed companies?" I must educate myself on those things.

Gladly, the information is available online. But for you, I will list my notes here for ease of reference and quick info. No need to do Google, Yahoo, or Bing. I have done that for you. Just stay on this book and keep on reading. This will save you time from pinching information from the internet. Not all information from internet are true, some of them are hoax. I have filtered that bad information for you. Also, you have saved precious money to pay for Internet café fees. Save that money to invest instead.

"Are you ready?" Open up your mind to the possibility of new information so these will easily be stored in your mind. Make your mind as a sponge so these facts will cling and easily understood. Rest assured that I have chosen words that is easy for you to understand and comprehend.

You can also go back to this chapter from time to time if ever you forgot some of the information. This will serve as your personal notes on investing.

For those already familiar with the information in this chapter, you can either skip or read it fast as sort of skimming to review the information. But I do suggest that you read this chapter at least once. You will never know what golden idea or fact you will come across.

What is Stock Market?

The Stock Market is where shares are issued and traded either through exchanges or over-the-counter.

What is the Philippine Stock Exchange?

Philippine Stock Exchange (PSE) facilitates the buying and selling of stocks and other securities through its accredited stock brokers or trading participants. Website is www.pse.com.ph.

What is a stock broker?

A stock broker is an agent or a firm who is a trading member of the stock exchange that executes the buying and selling of submitted orders by the investors. In doing so, the stock broker charges for a fee or commission for the transaction and its services.

Online brokers, also called discount brokers, offers online trading system for order submission.

What is an Online Trading System?

Online Trading System is submission of orders through the internet or mobile phone apps.

What is Securities and Exchange Commission?

Securities and Exchange Commission (SEC) is a government agency whose Primary mission is to protect investors and maintain the integrity of the capital markets, among which is the stock market.

What is a stock certificate?

Stock Certificate is piece of paper that certifies a person's share ownership in a corporation.

HOW TO INVEST IN THE PHILIPPINE STOCK MARKET

What is a Ticker?

Ticker is a computerized listing of information showing stock market activity and stock price movements. Information includes the stock symbol, last traded price and the volume of shares traded.

What are the type of Transactions accepted by PSE?

Type of transactions: Limit Order, Market Order, Good-til-cancelled order and Day order.

Limit order are orders placed to buy or sell shares of stock at a specified buying or selling price.

Market order are orders placed to buy or sell shares of stock at current market price.

Good-til-cancelled order are orders placed to buy or sell shares of stock that remains outstanding for seven calendar days until cancelled by the investor or trader.

Day order are orders placed to buy or sell shares of stock that is only valid for one trading day.

What are Bid and Ask Prices?

Bid Price is the highest price that a buyer is willing and able to purchase for a share of stock.

Ask price is the lowest price that a seller is willing and able to offer for sale for a share of stock. It is also called the "offer price".

What is PSEi?

PSE Composite Index (PSEi) is the benchmark index measuring the performance of the Philippine stock market. It is a fixed basket comprised of 30 listed companies representing the general movement of stock prices.

STEP 3 SELECT THE STOCK BROKER

"Give it to me! Show me the money!" I am now fired up. I could already see myself receiving the passive income that will be generated by my stock investments. I can now see my dreams achieved and keeps me motivated. But first, I must act. I need a stock broker.

As mentioned in chapter 2 Know the Facts, you need a stock broker to place orders to the stock exchange. The stock broker executes your buy and sell orders. This person or firm will be your partner to success. Just like in marriage, you need a partner that supports your success.

I am blessed with my wife, Grace for being supportive of my investing and especially in writing of this book. She is always on my side and helps me in my journey in life and goals. She is also one of my motivations. Our four year old boy John, I am learning stocks investment so I can teach him someday about it. I am also writing this book for him as his guide when in the future; he is ready to start investing in the Philippine Stock Market.

Having a supportive broker can provide you with the necessary functionalities needed to execute your stock order in timely submission and seamless transaction. "What do I need from my broker?" I was pondering this question so I can set criteria in selecting my stock broker.

I prefer that broker who provides online trading systems. I can submit my stock buy and sell orders online through the broker's website or through mobile phone using mobile applications. For me, online trading system must have these basic functions for:

- Order submission to buy, sell, withdraw, and amend orders.
- Order status viewing if orders are accepted, cancelled, amended, done partially or done all
- Portfolio viewing
- Transaction history viewing
- Price Updates
- Watch list monitoring
- Market and Index Information collection
- Market and Listed Company News updates
- Listed Company Financial Reports collection
- Charting and tools for technical analysis
- Market Research and Investment Guide
- Tutorials on Investing

I myself have developed and maintained systems for online web trading. I am well familiar with the technical design, technologies and protocols used. Before I was into stock investing, I am a software engineer with exposure to Online Trading Platforms. Having technical exposure is however different from investing knowledge, as I came to realize. But still, I could evaluate an online trading system based on my previous finance industry exposure which is mostly developing those online systems for trading.

After reviewing those listed online brokers, I observed that PSE itself and the brokers lack the functionality of Triggered Orders like Stop Loss, Trailing Stop, and Trigger Buy. However, there is a facility for Off-Hours orders. Some have Foreign Exchange rates, Bank Interest Rates, Gold and Commodities Information, and Bond Information. If you are investor who wants to cover all bases, you will need information on those other investment vehicles.

I chose COL Financial (formerly, Citisec) as my stock broker. After evaluating the available online brokers, COL was the one that closely fits to my needs. But for you, you will probably realize that COL is not for you and another one better fits your needs. The importance here is that you have done the selection of your broker after a thorough evaluation and that it is your decision to choose that online broker.

"What do I expect to have in my online broker?" Make a list of criteria that you wish to have in a broker. You can copy my list and add more on it. Or you can make a different set of criteria. Important thing is you have a set of items to check that will guide you to decide your online broker.

What are the list of online brokers to choose from?

From the PSE website, here are the listed qualified online brokers:

- AB CAPITAL SECURITIES, INC. (www.abcapitalsecurities.com.ph)
- ABACUS SECURITES CORP. (www.abacusonline.com.ph)
- ACCORD CAPITAL EQUITIES CORP. (www.accordcapital.ph)
- ANGPING & ASSOCIATES SECURITIES, INC. (www.angpingonline.com)
- BPI TRADE (www.bpitrade.com)
- COL FINANCIAL (www.colfinancial.com)
- F. YAP SECURITIES, INC. (www.2tradeasia.com)
- FIRST METRO SECURITIES (www.firstmetrosec.com.ph)
- RCBC SECURITIES, INC. (www.rcbcsec.com)
- WEALTH SECURITIES, INC. (www.wealthsec.net)

Browse through their website and using your criteria, evaluate their trading systems. Most of these brokers provide online tutorial to using the online systems. Some provide free trial use, and help line to discuss the features. Make most of these free to evaluate options and check with which online broker fits your needs.

I have selected online broker _____. Fill up the name of broker.

STEP 4 APPLY FOR A TRADING ACCOUNT

COL is for me. I made a decision to open a trading account with COL Financials. I went to their website link for Opening an Account, prepared the necessary documents, filled up the forms and sent those requirements to COL Financial in postal mail. After funding my trading account, I can now submit my orders to PSE. Yahooooo!

I will guide you to the details of the simple steps of opening a trading account with your broker. The process is simple and the shortest depending on your communication with your broker. The earlier you submit the documents, the earlier the broker can process your account opening request. These brokers are working on typical Philippine working days Monday to Friday 8 AM to 5 PM. Some can process your request at least 3 working days from receipt of your documents. For faster communication, you can provide them with your email address to contact you.

What are the requirements to open a trading account?

After selecting your online broker, go to their website and check the page on opening your first trading account with them. Take note of the requirements if you can collect and provide to them.

Select the right trading account type to open. Most of the brokers have Individual or Corporate accounts. Some of them offers an Easy Investment Plan trading accounts or similar type. You can start with the Easy Investment Plan as these trading accounts do not require a big investment. You can start with Five Thousand Pesos that you will save monthly and invest to a planned set of listed companies to buy. This type of account allows you to initially be exposed to investing. If you prefer to do it on your own, you can upgrade to Individual trading accounts and top up your trading deposit amount.

Basically, these brokers will ask for proof of identity. Passport, Company or Government Identification cards will do. Check also if they accept for foreign investor trading accounts. Another set of identification might be required for foreigners opening trading accounts.

For every account type, there is a corresponding funding requirement. To start with, select the account type that you can easily afford. This account will jumpstart you to invest. If you can afford for bigger trading amounts or became sophisticated investor, you can always upgrade your account type anytime.

Each broker has set of forms for you to fill up. Download these opening forms from broker's website. Fill up those forms and send to them. I would suggest to send those documents through postal. Some of them need the forms with your actual signatures. Digital signature is not yet mostly accepted industry practice in the Philippines.

How do you fund your Trading Account?

Once your application is pre-approved, customer service personnel will contact you through your email address for the funding details. If something is missing on your application, they will also notify you so you can proceed with the application approval.

Funding your trading account can be done through:

- Online Bills Payment from accepted major banks accepted
- Over-the-Counter Bills Payment from accepted major banks
- Business Center
- Overseas Remittance

Since I have a Metrobank account in the Philippines, I can use the Online Bills Payment of Metrobank online web banking system to pay the deposit for my trading account. Once COL has confirmed receiving the bill payment, they will update your trading account's available funds for trading. You can see this in the portfolio view of the online trading system.

You can select from the payment modes available from your broker to fund your trading account. I also include this feature in my criteria in selecting the broker so in the future deposits, it will be easy for me to immediately fund my portfolio.

For those opening the Easy Investment Program, you also need to make the deposit worry free on your part as you need to deposit periodically to fund the planned stock purchase.

Let the trading begins! But wait, you have only have accomplished the technicality side of preparation to trade. Just like setting up a new TV, after you plug the power cord, turned on the power, you can now watch movies from the available channels. But which channel to set is not yet done. These stocks to buy and when to exit from an open position is not yet done. You need to plan out your trade.

I invite you to continue reading and discover the different trading strategies that you can use on your trading plan. A general without a battle plan has already lost the battle from the start. It is better to have a plan and lost, than lost without a plan. Those having a plan can always tweak the plan so as not to repeat the mistakes. Those without a plan has nothing to go back and improve. Most of these people who trades with no plan will quit. And we know, "Quitters never win. Winners never quit."

STEP 5 MAKE A TRADING PLAN

My wife Grace has started investing with COL through their Easy Investment Plan. She invested Five Thousand Pesos to buy from the listed suggested stocks. The experience of having a plan to invest stocks have taught her that she must have a plan before trading. Hers was the EIP plan. Mine was different. Yours might be different. But the important thing is that you must have a trading plan that you have faith in it and must have the discipline to follow it.

Grace is the one who introduces me to stock investing. I was very thankful for her as I am really looking for ways to invest. We usually compare notes on our trades done but since we have different trading paradigms, we can only check the behavior of the stocks and not the trading plan.

You will have your own trading plan and this might be different from others. Everyone has its own style, own way to conduct its trades, own trading plan. We have to respect that and try to evaluate which ones are giving more profitable results. We never know, we can use their methods and be profitable also.

For those starting with the EIP or similar type of trading plan. This chapter will be educational for you on some strategies that you can apply when you plan to setup your own trading plan. But for now, follow the EIP plan until you will have confidence to start out yourselves.

My plan is to start out as technical investor focusing on short-term day with trading funding of One hundred thousand pesos to start. I would like to grow this starting fund in a year for at least 20%. When I feel more confident, I can top up the amount. In the future once I reached millions to invest, I might prefer to be fundamental investor choosing companies based on their financial health.

I am currently using trading system similar to T3B (www.t3bsystem.com) system. Some details of my trading I could not divulge as most of it is personal and some are proprietary.

To formulate your own trading plan, I will list out those strategies available that you can use or mixed use with other trading strategies. Our goal here is to formulate a trading plan that we can follow. A trading plan that is simple to understand on your part. Easy to implement. A plan that provides more profit for trades. And a plan that includes exit strategy to avoid big losses.

Are you a Fundamental or Technical investor?

A Fundamental investor is a follower of Fundamental Analysis. A Technical investor is a follower of Technical Analysis.

What is Fundamental Analysis?

Fundamental Analysis is a method of evaluating a security that entails attempting to measure its intrinsic value by examining related economic, financial and other qualitative and quantitative factors. Fundamental analysts attempt to study everything that can affect the security's value, including macroeconomic factors (like the overall economy and industry conditions) and company-specific factors (like financial condition and management).

The end goal of performing fundamental analysis is to produce a value that an investor can compare with the security's current price, with the aim of figuring out what sort of position to take with that security (underpriced – buy, overpriced = sell or short).

One of the proponents of Fundamental Analysis is Warren Buffet. With his introduction of Value Investing strategy which mostly is using the fundamental tools for analysis.

As a Fundamental analyst, you will check first the company for Qualitative factors like:
- What is the Business Model?

- What is its competitive edge?
- Who are in the Management Team?
- How good is the Corporate Governance?

Then, check the Qualitative factors of the Industry where the company is doing its core business:
- Customers
- Market Share
- Industry Growth
- Competition
- Regulation

The fundamental analyst must be familiar with the industry and the companies within the industry. And finally select the company or group of companies he thinks passed the qualitative factors.

The fundamental analyst will go to the details of the company's financial reports or statement:
- Balance Sheets
- Income Statement
- Statement of Cash Flows
- SEC filing and disclosures

He will look the following items in a financial report:
- Management Discussion and Analysis (MD&A)
- The Auditor's Report
- Notes to Financial Statements
- Accounting Methods
- Disclosures

Although most Fundamental Analyst perform a thorough reading and research on those listed items, their evaluation somehow differs from each other. And even how to compute the intrinsic value of a company based on fundamentals differs from one analyst to another.

What is Technical Analysis?

Technical Analysis is a method of evaluating securities by analyzing statistics generated by market activity, such as past prices and volume. The technical analysts do not attempt to measure security's intrinsic value, but instead use charts and other tools to identify patterns that can suggest future activity.

The field of Technical Analysis is based on three assumptions:
1. The Market Discounts Everything
2. Price Moves in Trends
3. History Tends to Repeat Itself

Three Types of Trends:
- Uptrends
- Downtrends
- Sideways/Horizontal Trends

Trendline is a simple charting technique that adds a line to a chart to represent the trend in the market or a stock. Channel lines is the addition of two parallel trendlines that act as strong areas of support and resistance.

It is important to be able to understand and identify trends so you can trade with rather than against them. Two important sayings in technical analysis are "The trend is your friend" and "Don't buck the trend".

Support and resistance analysis is an important part of trends because it can be used to make trading decisions and identify when a trend is reversing. So if you are bullish on a stock that is moving toward an important support level, do not place the trade at the support level. Instead, place it above the support level, but within a few points. On the other hand, if you are placing stops or short selling, set up the trade price at or below the level of support.

A chart is simply a graphical representation of a series of prices over a set time frame. A chart has time scale that varies from decades to seconds. Most frequently used time scales are intraday, daily weekly, monthly, quarterly and annually.

Types of Charts:
- Line chart
- Bar chart
- Candlestick chart
- Point and Figure Charts

Candlestick chart is similar to bar chart, but differs in a way it is visually constructed. There are two color constructs for days up and one for days that the price falls. When the price of the stock is up and closes above the opening trade, the candlestick is usually be white or clear. If the stock has traded down for the period, then the candlestick will usually be red or black.

In the chart, we can look for patterns that resembles with the common studied patterns and be able to trade accordingly with these patterns:
- Head and Shoulders
- Cup and Handle
- Double Tops and Bottoms
- Triangles: symmetrical, ascending and descending
- Flag and Pennant
- Wedge
- Gaps
- Triple Tops and Bottoms
- Rounding Bottom

Moving Average is the average price of a security over a set amount of time. Types of Moving Averages:
- Simple Moving Average (SMA) – Sum of all of the past closing prices over the time period and divides the result by the number of prices used in the calculation.
- Linear Weighted Average – Sum of all the closing prices over a certain time period and multiplying them by the position of the data point and then dividing by the sum of the number of periods.
- Exponential Moving Average (EMA) – Uses a smoothing factor to place a higher weight on recent data points

Moving averages are used to identify current trends and trend reversals as well as to set up support and resistance levels. It can be used to quickly identify whether a security is moving in an uptrend or a downtrend depending on its direction of the moving average. Another signal of trend reversal is when one moving average crosses through another.

Indicators are calculations based on the price and the volume of a security that measure such things as money, flow, trends, volatility and momentum. Oscillators are momentum indicators.

A list of indicators and oscillators:
- Accumulation/Distribution Line
- Average Directional Index (ADX)
- Aroon

- Aroon Oscillator
- Moving Average Convergence Divergence (MACD)
- Relative Strength Index (RSI)
- On-Balance Volume (OBV)
- Stochastic Oscillator

Are you a Fundamental investor? How do you evaluate the stocks based on intrinsic value? Which group of stocks with strong Fundamentals?

Are you instead a Technical investor? What day trading system are you using to enter and exit a position?

Whatever trading plan will it be, keep it documented for you to review during your trade sessions. Tweak it if possible based on your new learning and ideas. Keep it simple. Keep it safe. It is your trade secret.

STEP 6 START TRADING

We have ventured far and now you are ready to make that big leap forward to submit your first trade. Go ahead.

Remember to always keep motivated to invest. Save to invest. Pay yourself first. Follow the trend and stick to your trading plan.

You will make mistakes on some of your trades. Be thankful, it is a learning process. Avoid those mistakes by tweaking your plan.

I have setup a blog site philstocknews.blogspot.sg for you so we can share our ideas on trades and experiences. I invite you to visit the blog for more updates on Philippine stock market and revision editions of this book. I plan to make future editions of this book as the trading market changes.

It has been a great pleasure for me to be of assistance in your first step towards investing in the Philippine Stock Market.

Happy Trading!

ABOUT THE AUTHOR

Elton John T. Aguilar is software engineer with years of experience and exposure to Online Trading Systems. Industry exposure from Web Trading Systems, Web Data Distribution System, Order Management System, Price Feed and Feeder Systems.

He is also actively trading in the Philippine Stock Exchange. He maintains an online blog PhilStockNews.blogspot.sg that monitors the current market trends of the Philippines and PSE.

Graduated with Bachelor of Science in Computer Science in University of San Carlos and holds a degree of Master of Science in Information Technology at Ateneo de Manila University.

He is also a professor, book author, technical thesis advisor and a chess enthusiast.

www.ingramcontent.com/pod-product-compliance
Lightning Source LLC
Chambersburg PA
CBHW061522180526
45171CB00001B/298